EXPLORING CIVIL RIGHTS

THE RISE

1978

NEL YOMTOV

Franklin Watts®
An imprint of Scholastic Inc.

Content Consultant

A special thank you to Ryan M. Jones at the
National Civil Rights Museum for his expert consultation.

Library of Congress Cataloging-in-Publication Data
Names: Yomtov, Nel, author.
Title: The rise: 1978 / Nel Yomtov.
Other titles: Exploring civil rights.
Description: First edition. | New York : Franklin Watts, an imprint of
    Scholastic Inc., 2023. | Series: Exploring civil rights | Includes
    bibliographical references and index. | Audience: Ages 10–14. |
    Audience: Grades 7–9. | Summary: "Series continuation. Narrative
    nonfiction, key events of the Civil Rights Movement in the years after
    1965. Photographs throughout"—Provided by publisher.
Identifiers: LCCN 2022039999 (print) | LCCN 2022040000 (ebook) |
    ISBN 9781338837650 (library binding) | ISBN 9781338837667 (paperback) |
    ISBN 9781338837674 (ebk)
Subjects: LCSH: African Americans—Civil rights—History—20th
    century—Juvenile literature. | Civil rights movements—United
    States—History—20th century—Juvenile literature. | Civil rights
    workers—United States—Juvenile literature. | BISAC: JUVENILE
    NONFICTION / Social Topics / Civil & Human Rights | JUVENILE NONFICTION
    / History / General
Classification: LCC E185.615 .Y56 2023 (print) | LCC E185.615 (ebook) |
    DDC 323.1196/073—dc23/eng/20220823
LC record available at https://lccn.loc.gov/2022039999
LC ebook record available at https://lccn.loc.gov/2022040000

10 9 8 7 6 5 4 3 2 1   23 24 25 26 27

Printed in China   62
First edition, 2023

Composition by Kay Petronio

COVER & TITLE PAGE:
Supporters of the Equal
Rights Amendment
march in Washington,
DC, in July 1978.

Students at the University of California, Berkeley, page 42.

Table of Contents

Mayor Kenneth A. Gibson, page 11.

A segregated bus terminal with a sign reading "White Waiting Room" in Memphis, Tennessee, in 1943.

The Way It Was

The year 1865 was an important one in U.S. history. The American Civil War (1861–1865) ended and the Thirteenth **Amendment** to the U.S. Constitution was passed, **abolishing** slavery. This period of time also introduced Black codes in the form of **Jim Crow** laws. These laws restricted where people of color could live and work and were especially strict in the American South.

Jim Crow laws enforced **segregation**. Under the racial policy of "separate but equal," Black Americans could be given access to separate facilities if their quality was equal to that of white facilities. In reality, however, there was no equality. African Americans were forced to attend separate and inadequate schools and live in run-down neighborhoods.

The Fight Begins

As Jim Crow practices continued, two prominent **civil rights** organizations emerged. The National Association of Colored Women's Clubs (NACWC) was founded in 1896 by a group of politically active women, including Harriet Tubman. Members of the association dedicated themselves to fighting for voting rights and for ending racial violence in the form of **lynchings** against African Americans.

The National Association for the Advancement of Colored People (NAACP), founded in 1909, followed in the NACWC's footsteps. The NAACP focused on opposing segregation and Jim Crow policies. Both organizations would be crucial in the coming fight for justice.

Lasting Changes

In the following years, the Great Depression (1929–1939) and World War II (1939–1945) left Black Americans fighting for their lives at home and overseas. The 1954 U.S. Supreme Court decision in the *Brown v. Board of Education of Topeka* case challenging school segregation finally put an end to "separate but equal" in public schools. The years between 1955 and 1965 would serve as the heart of the civil rights movement. Rosa Parks refused to give up her seat on a bus, sparking the Montgomery bus **boycott**. The Reverend Dr. Martin Luther King, Jr., emerged as a leader and organized the March on Washington for Jobs and Freedom, the largest civil rights demonstration at the time.

The 1960s and 1970s further ignited those yearning for equal opportunities under the law. **Activists** continued to persevere, resulting in lasting changes for the African American community.

1978

The year 1978 was one of steps toward equality. In this book, learn how Max Robinson successfully became the first African American broadcast network anchor for ABC News. Read about how the Supreme Court case *Regents of the University of California v. Bakke* ruled that **affirmative action** was legal in the United States and race could be included in the criteria for admissions into colleges and universities. And discover how the National Organization of Women (NOW) coordinated an impressive march of 100,000 demonstrators in Washington, DC, in support of the Equal Rights Amendment. ■

Demonstrators carry a banner at the Equal Rights Amendment march in Washington, DC.

Mayor Maynard Jackson was elected the first Black mayor of Atlanta, Georgia, in 1973.

1

An Era of Groundbreakers

The efforts of the civil rights activists in the 1960s were rewarded with important **legislation** that changed the face of America. The Civil Rights Act of 1964 outlawed racial **discrimination** in public places, **federally** funded programs, and the workplace. The Voting Rights Act of 1965 **prohibited** racial discrimination in voting. As the 1960s drew to an end, the Fair Housing Act of 1968 outlawed discrimination in housing sales, rentals, and financing.

These legislative victories had a significant impact on the lives of Black Americans. The new laws began the process of breaking down barriers in job segregation, opening the door to better-paying jobs and benefits. With equal access to the voting booth, Black urban and rural communities gained political representation as never before. By 1973, 43 African Americans served as mayor in cities throughout the country. By 1977, more than 200 cities had Black mayors.

The 1970s: A New Era

In what historians call the start of the post–civil rights movement era, the 1970s marked the beginning of a new chapter in the struggle for civil rights. The decade saw Black Americans making vital political, business, and academic progress. In 1970, Dr. Clifton Wharton, Jr., was named as president of Michigan State University, becoming the first African American to lead a mainly white college in the 20th century. The same year, Kenneth A. Gibson was elected the first Black mayor of Newark,

Dr. Clifton Wharton, Jr., in his office in New York City in 1969.

Mayor Kenneth A. Gibson in Newark, New Jersey, in 1970.

New Jersey, one of the nation's major shipping and transportation hubs.

Important civil rights gains were made on the national political scene. In March 1971, Black members of the U.S. House of Representatives founded the Congressional Black Caucus (CBC). Its goal was to promote the welfare of African Americans through legislation ranging from employment to welfare reform and health care. In 1972, New York Congresswoman Shirley Chisholm became the first African American woman to campaign for the presidential nomination of the Democratic Party. Though she lost her bid, Chisholm—one of the founders of the CBC—would represent her New York district in Congress until 1983.

Arthur Ashe hoists the championship trophy at the 1975 Wimbledon Championships.

During the decade, Black Americans also achieved noteworthy "firsts" in literature and sports. In August 1970, playwright Charles Gordone won the Pulitzer Prize in Drama for the play *No Place to Be Somebody*. Gordone was the first African American playwright to receive a Pulitzer. The play focused on racial tensions during the civil rights era in New York City. In 1975, tennis great Arthur Ashe bested Jimmy Connors to become the first Black person to win the men's singles title at Wimbledon, the world's most **prestigious** championship in tennis.

Many more significant achievements in the civil rights movement would grab the headlines in 1978.

Shirley Chisholm on the campaign trail during her 1972 presidential bid.

Literary Greatness

On January 11, 1978, Toni Morrison won the
National Book Critics Circle Award (NBCC) for her
third novel, *Song of Solomon.* The NBCC awards
are American literary honors given every year to
promote "the finest books and reviews in English."
Though Morrison's two previous works, *The Bluest
Eye* (1969) and *Sula* (1973), were well received by
critics and readers, *Song of Solomon* brought the
47-year-old author national fame and recognition
for the first time. The story follows the life of
Macon "Milkman" Dead III, a Black man **alienated**
from his family and his African cultural roots.

National Book
Critics Circle Award winner
Toni Morrison in 1978.

The Year in Entertainment

Notable Black and **Latino** entertainers made their mark on popular culture in 1978. On April 7, Prince released his first album, *For You*. Prince would release 42 studio albums and four live albums, and rack up sales of more than 150 million records worldwide. On September 17, **Latina** performer Rita Moreno won an Emmy Award at the 30th Primetime Emmy Awards ceremony for her performance in an episode of the police drama *The Rockford Files*. On September 18, *WKRP in Cincinnati* premiered. The TV sitcom starred African American actor Tim Reid as radio disc jockey Venus Flytrap. The TV sitcom *Diff'rent Strokes* premiered on November 3. The popular series starred Black actors Gary Coleman and Todd Bridges as two African American boys adopted by a rich white businessman.

Rita Moreno poses with her Emmy at the 30th Primetime Emmy Awards.

Tim Reid as radio disc jockey Venus Flytrap, on *WKRP in Cincinnati*.

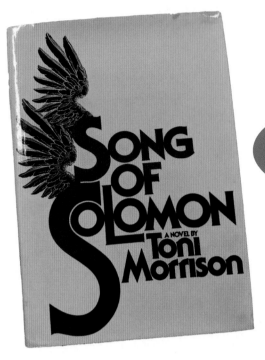

Song of Solomon is also based on an African American folktale in which a Black man escapes enslavement by flying back to Africa.

Song of Solomon was chosen as a main selection of the Book-of-the-Month Club, the first novel by a Black author to be chosen since 1940. More than 500,000 copies of the novel have been sold worldwide, and it has been translated into 10 languages. Throughout her career, Morrison wrote almost exclusively about Black life and culture. The legacy of slavery and its impact on Black Americans dominated her writings. "I simply wanted to write literature that was irrevocably, indisputably Black," she said.

Diversity in the Courts

The federal court system made a giant stride toward increased **diversity** when President Jimmy Carter nominated Jack Tanner to a seat on the U.S. District Court for the Western District of Washington on January 20. The Senate confirmed Tanner in May 1978, making him the first African American federal judge in the northwest United States. Ten years earlier, Tanner had assumed another role as barrier breaker, becoming the first African American in Washington State history to run for governor. Judge Tanner was known for his civil rights activism and his belief that the court system should be a place of justice and equality regardless of race, gender, or social class.

Judge Jack Tanner.

Children's Rights

On February 7, 1978, Poland proposed to the United Nations (UN) the idea of a treaty, or agreement, to protect the civil, political, **economic**, social, and health rights of children worldwide. The UN is a global organization whose purpose is to maintain international peace and security. Poland raised the issue as the UN planned programs that would take place in 1979 during a campaign called the International Year of the Child. A UN group was formed to write the treaty, called the Convention on the Rights of the Child (CRC). The UN officially adopted the CRC on November 20, 1989. Today the CRC requires nations to report the status of children's welfare in their nation to the UN every five years.

Jean Young and comedian Danny Kaye display the poster proclaiming 1979 as the International Year of the Child.

Fly the Friendly Skies

The National Aeronautics and Space Administration (NASA) made big headlines when it announced the 1978 Astronaut Class on January 16. The group included America's first women astronauts: Sally Ride, Judith Resnick, Kathryn Sullivan, Shannon Lucid, Anna Fisher, and Margaret Rhea Seddon. Ride would become the first American woman in space, while Resnick was the first Jewish American astronaut. The 1978 Astronaut Class also included the first African Americans in NASA's space program, Guion "Guy" Bluford and Fred Gregory. Bluford became the first African American in space, as a crewmember of the space shuttle *Challenger* in 1983.

Guion "Guy" Bluford prepares for his 1983 mission aboard Space Shuttle *Challenger*.

Broadcast News

In February, trailblazing journalist Max Robinson became the first Black person to anchor the nightly network news, on ABC's *World News Tonight*. Robinson had previously won awards for his coverage of the 1968 civil rights uprising after the assassination of Dr. King. At ABC, Robinson frequently clashed with management, claiming news stories portrayed Black Americans unfairly. He left ABC in 1984 to become the first Black anchor at a local station in Chicago. Robinson later taught at colleges on the East Coast. Robinson cofounded the National Association of Black Journalists and influenced many future Black anchors, including Ed Bradley and Lester Holt. ▪

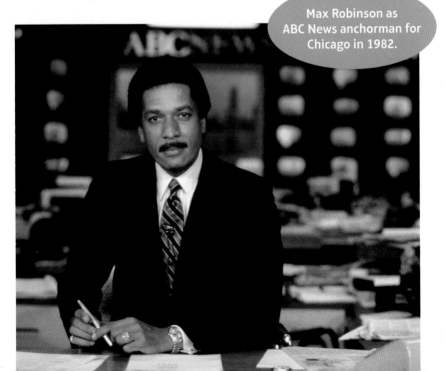

Max Robinson as ABC News anchorman for Chicago in 1982.

Karen DeCrow,
president of the
National Organization
for Women in 1977.

The Gathering Crowds

By the mid 1970s, the issue of women's rights had taken center stage on the political and social scene in the United States. The women's rights movement, also called the women's **liberation** movement, worked for equal rights and opportunities for women. Women's activist organizations such as the National Organization for Women viewed themselves as the women's equivalent of the NAACP. By the late 1970s, advances were made in women's access to education, an increased role in politics, and better job opportunities and higher wages. Every March, people in the United States celebrate Women's History Month in recognition of the achievements and contributions of women to society.

A Celebration of Women

Women's History Month originated in March 1978 when the Education Task Force of the Sonoma County Commission on the Status of Women declared "Women's History Week" in Santa Rosa, California. The week included International Women's Day, March 8, which had been recognized globally since the early 20th century. The Sonoma County Commission had been formed in 1975 to

CELEBRATES
TORY WEEK

The Sonoma County women's movement planted the seeds for Women's History Month.

fight **prejudice** and gender discrimination. One of its aims was to help the county **comply** with Title IX of the Education Amendments of 1972. This law prohibited gender discrimination by schools receiving aid from the federal government.

The commission feared that a lack of educational materials about women's history in Sonoma schools violated the law, and therefore risked losing

Molly Murphy MacGregor (left) poses with her cofounders of the National Women's History Project.

federal aid. In response, the commission convinced the community to host a women's history week. The first-of-its-kind Women's History Week was celebrated with a parade, workshops, and educational materials for local schools. The celebration made national headlines. Within months, women from around the country began to push for a celebration of women's history and achievements on a larger scale. In early 1980, Molly Murphy MacGregor—a Sonoma County teacher and organizer of the March 1978 celebration—and others created the National Women's History Project (NWHP) to achieve the goal.

The NWHP distributed classroom materials to teachers across the country about women's achievements and their important role in history. The organization also pressed Congress and the White House to celebrate and recognize women's role in history every year. The group's efforts paid off. In 1980, President Carter declared the week of March 8 National Women's History Week. The weeklong event became a monthlong one in 1987 by an act of Congress and has been celebrated every March since. The local celebration in a small California town in March 1978 had blossomed into a national celebration.

President Jimmy Carter signs the document establishing National Women's History Week.

Protesting Apartheid

In February, the UN adopted a **resolution** to establish the International Anti-**Apartheid** Year, 1978–1979. On March 18, 2,000 Black civil rights activists marched in Nashville, Tennessee, from the state capitol to Vanderbilt University. The university was the site of a white South African tennis team playing a U.S. team in a major tournament. The marchers were protesting South Africa's anti-Black racial policies. Many of the marchers were university students participating in their first human rights protest. International pressure and determined resistance by Black South Africans against apartheid eventually led to its downfall in the early 1990s.

Anti-apartheid protesters gather at Vanderbilt University in Nashville, Tennessee.

Muhammad Ali (center) addresses the UN Special Committee Against Racism.

The Champ Speaks

South Africa's system of legal segregation known as apartheid was a target of human rights activists in early 1978. On April 8, anti-apartheid activist and former heavyweight boxing champion Muhammad Ali addressed the United Nations at a session of the Special Committee Against Apartheid. Ali delivered a powerful message of peace and spirituality to representatives from nations around the world. He said that having a loving, merciful heart was the way to achieve international brotherhood. Ali continued to speak out against apartheid throughout his life. One of the world's most prominent figures, his words inspired countless people.

A button created by the NAACP for the anti-apartheid march in Nashville, TN.

Groundbreaking Theater

On April 20, the play *Zoot Suit* premiered at the Mark Taper Forum in Los Angeles, California. Luis Valdez wrote the play with music by Daniel Valdez and Lalo Guerrero. *Zoot Suit* is based on the Zoot Suit Riots in Los Angeles in 1943. The term "zoot suit" refers to a style of men's clothing that became popular in Latino, African American, and other minority communities across the United States during the 1940s. The style featured baggy high-waisted pants and a long coat with wide lapels and heavily padded shoulders.

On the evening of May 30, 1943, a band of white sailors and soldiers stationed around Los Angeles attacked a group of Latino youth. One sailor was injured, sparking a series of violent clashes between white servicemen, police officers, and **civilians** with young Latinos.

The Chicano Movement

The Zoot Suit Riots gave birth to a new generation of civil rights activists. One result of their activism was the **Chicano** Movement, a civil rights crusade by Mexican Americans. The movement pressed for social and political advancement and recognition. Chicano student groups staged school walkouts and **sit-ins** in cities throughout the country. The protests brought attention to high Chicano school dropout rates and a second-rate education system in schools with a large Chicano student body. Chicano activism led to more bilingual education programs in U.S. public schools and a Supreme Court ruling that made it illegal to prevent non-English speakers from receiving an education.

Chicano activists call for more Chicano teachers in schools in Denver, Colorado.

Teens dressed in zoot suits in 1943.

Zoot Suiters under arrest outside a Los Angeles jail during the 1943 riots.

The Latinos were beaten, stripped of their zoot suits, and left bleeding on the streets. The rioting spread to nearby communities, as Filipinos and African Americans also became victims of the mob's violence. The Zoot Suit Riots ended on June 8. No sailors or soldiers were ever arrested in the beatings, although hundreds of Latinos were.

Zoot Suit was the first professionally produced Chicano, or Mexican American, play in the United States. Its 10-day run in April 1978 played to a

packed theater, earning standing ovations at the end
of each performance. A second sold-out run began
on August 17, 1978, and then played at the Aquarius
Theater in Hollywood. Nearly half a million people
saw *Zoot Suit* in Los Angeles in a year. The play
then moved to New York, where it became the first

The 1981 musical drama film *Zoot Suit* is an adaptation of the groundbreaking play.

Chicano theatrical production to be performed on Broadway. "No other Latino play has had the cultural impact of *Zoot Suit*," wrote Robert Ito in the *New York Times* about a revival of the play in 2017. ∎

100 YEARS EARLIER

John "Bud" Fowler made his first documented appearance in an exhibition game in April 1878, pitching for a non-professional ball club from Chelsea, Massachusetts. He was the first professional African American baseball player and the first to play on **integrated** teams. Fowler was born John W. Jackson, Jr., in 1858, in Fort Plain, New York. For unknown reasons, he changed his last name. Fowler grew up in nearby Cooperstown, where he learned to play baseball on the fields of the local church. After his first game, Fowler continued to play with Chelsea over the next few weeks.

Bud Fowler (last row, center) with teammates of the Keokuk, Iowa, baseball team, in 1885.

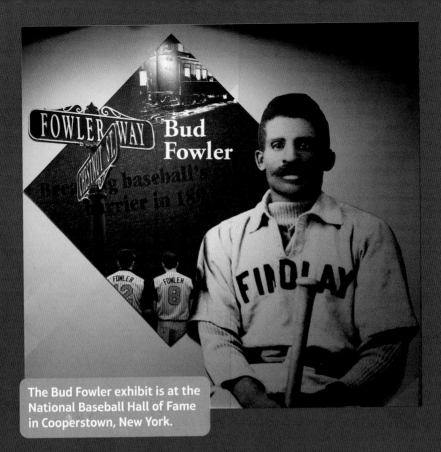

The Bud Fowler exhibit is at the National Baseball Hall of Fame in Cooperstown, New York.

Fowler caught the attention of the International Association, a professional league formed in 1877. The Lynn Live Oaks invited Fowler to join their team. On May 17, 1878, Fowler took the mound against a team from Ontario, Canada, becoming the first Black ball-player to play professional baseball in the United States. Fowler played several more games with the Oaks, and then moved on to play with other teams in the Boston area and beyond. In a career that spanned nearly 30 years, Fowler played, managed, and promoted baseball in 22 U.S. states and Canada in at least 13 professional leagues. Bud Fowler died in 1913 at the age of 54.

Harvey Milk at the Gay Pride Parade in San Francisco on June 23, 1978.

Pride and Policy

June 1978 was a landmark time for the gay and minority rights movements. During the 18th,19th, and 20th centuries, homosexuality was a crime in many places across the United States. In the struggle for social equality and full legal rights, significant gains were made during the 1960s. U.S. cities and states began to pass **decriminalization** laws. For the first time, openly gay individuals were elected to public office. Gay rights marches and pride parades were held regularly in American communities, including a historic parade in June.

On June 25, the rainbow flag of the gay movement flew for the first time at the San Francisco Gay Freedom Day Parade. The parade had been held annually since 1970 to celebrate gay individuals. One of the goals of the June 25 parade was to gain voter support against a ban on gays and

The original eight-stripe rainbow flag waves in a windy sky.

lesbians from working in California schools. The ban was defeated in November 1978 following opposition by the gay community and its supporters.

Artist and activist Gilbert Baker, who was urged by city official Harvey Milk to create a symbol of pride for the gay community, designed the first version of the rainbow flag. Baker's first flag was eight colorful stripes symbolizing diversity and unity: hot pink, red, orange, yellow, green, turquoise, indigo, and violet. Baker sewed the two flags that flew in the parade on his sewing machine.

Gilbert Baker sewing rainbow flags for the 1998 Gay Pride Parade in San Francisco.

Harvey Milk outside his San Francisco camera shop in 1977.

Harvey Milk

Harvey Milk was one of the first openly gay elected officials in the United States. Milk moved to San Francisco from New York in 1972, where he became a leading spokesman for the local gay community. In 1977, Milk won a seat on the San Francisco Board of Supervisors. He was sworn into office on January 9, 1978. Milk championed gay rights, low-cost housing, day care centers, and other citizen-friendly issues. On November 27, 1978, a former city supervisor shot and killed Milk and San Francisco mayor George Moscone. Milk's life and work have been celebrated in films, books, plays, public school names, and a U.S. postage stamp.

The rainbow flag was officially adopted as the international symbol of gay pride in 1994. That year Baker designed a mile-long, 30-feet-wide rainbow flag that was carried by 10,000 people in a New York City gay rights parade. Baker's enormous flag represented a "continuous path of freedom," said parade organizers. Today the flag contains six stripes—red, orange, yellow, green, blue, and violet.

Expanding Civil Rights

By the early 1970s, many colleges and universities began to revise their admissions policy to include more minority students. Studies have shown that Black and Hispanic students routinely score lower on standardized tests as a result of economic inequality and poorer educational opportunities compared to

The University of California, Berkeley was the first campus of the University of California system.

Gilbert Baker raises the rainbow flag at a rally in Florida in 2003.

Allan Bakke attends his first day at the University of California, Davis.

white students. This policy was called affirmative action. The University of California, Davis, School of Medicine (UCD) had such a policy. The school had two admissions programs: the regular one and a program in which 16 out of 100 places were reserved for students the school labeled "Black," "Chicanos," "Asians," and "American Indians."

Admission Denied

In early 1972, Allan Bakke, a 32-year-old white man, applied to UCD. He was rejected. Bakke applied again in August 1973 and received his second rejection letter at the end of September. Bakke was angered. His academic qualifications, including his college grade point average (GPA) and test scores were higher than any of the minority students admitted to UCD in the two years his applications were rejected. Bakke decided to sue the school. He believed he was denied admission *solely* on the basis of race. Bakke claimed the special admissions policy violated the Constitution's Fourteenth Amendment, which guarantees that individuals in similar situations be equally treated by the law. He also claimed his rights were violated under the Civil Rights Act of 1964.

Bakke sued the University of California in a state court. The court agreed with Bakke, ruling that the school's policy discriminated against certain groups. The court concluded that "no applicant may be rejected because of his race, in favor of another who is less qualified." The court ordered UCD to end its policy and ordered Bakke to be admitted. In response, UCD appealed the decision to the U.S. Supreme Court.

The Final Decision

The Supreme Court issued its decision on June 26, 1978, in *Regents of the University of California v. Bakke*. The court ruled that UCD's policy racially discriminated against white applicants because it excluded them from 16 of 100 available spots based solely on their race. The court ruled the practice did indeed violate the Fourteenth Amendment.

Opponents of Bakke's lawsuit protest outside the Supreme Court in Washington, DC, in 1977.

But the court also ruled that the school had the right to correct past discrimination of minorities in its admission policies. UCD could use race in its admissions program to promote diversity—but only if race was one of many factors used in judging each applicant. The historic decision was a victory for both parties. Bakke was allowed to enroll at UCD—which he did on September 25, 1978—*and* the use of affirmative action was extended, benefitting racial minorities not only at UCD but also at schools across the country. ■

FIGHT NATIONAL OPPRESSION

SACRAMENTO / DAVIS

Keep Action

NO BICYCLE PARKING IN THIS AREA

WRESTLING

Demonstrators at the University of California protest Allan Bakke's arrival during the first day of classes.

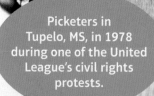

Support the
UNITED
LEAGUE'S
Just
struggl

Jea
Opp
We
Our

Black people
demand:
Political
Power

Picketers in
Tupelo, MS, in 1978
during one of the United
League's civil rights
protests.

4

Taking It to the Streets

The city of Tupelo, Mississippi, is on land that was once made up of **plantations** where enslaved Black people labored in cotton fields. In a state known for its racial hostilities, Tupelo seemed to have escaped the racial unrest and violence that swept across most of Mississippi during the 1960s. "Race relations here are excellent," wrote a *Washington Post* reporter about the town that called itself "The All-American City."

Summer of Discontent

Then in the summer of 1978, civil rights protests began. The seeds of the protests were planted in the summer of 1976 in an incident of police brutality. Eugene Pastro, a Black man, was arrested by Tupelo police on charges of cashing

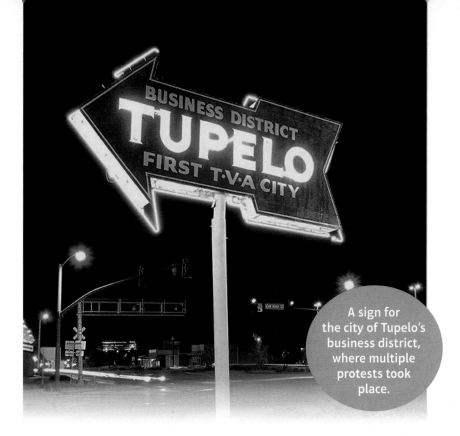

A sign for the city of Tupelo's business district, where multiple protests took place.

a bad check. Pastro was sent to prison in Atlanta, where he claimed he had been severely beaten by police in Tupelo. Months passed. Pastro sued the city. The court found two policemen guilty of brutality and fined them $2,500 each. The city refused to fire the two men, and a police review board found them not guilty. Members of the Black community were frustrated and angry.

The Boycott Begins

In response to the city's refusal to fire the officers, the United League of Mississippi, a civil rights organization, mounted a Black boycott of Tupelo's white-owned businesses. The boycott started on March 24, 1978, and had an immediate negative effect on stores' sales. The city reacted by first suspending the officers for two weeks. But the boycott continued. Black citizens began to **picket** white-owned shops and march in protest, forcing Tupelo to transfer the two officers to the city's fire department.

Many white citizens of Tupelo were angered by the boycott and marches. On May 6, members of the **Ku Klux Klan** (KKK), a white supremacist group, launched a countermarch. KKK leaders threatened to arrest the Black protesters. Armed Klansmen drove past Black picketers, jeering and hurling racial insults.

Members of the KKK confront a Black man during the boycott in Tupelo.

The protesters began to arm themselves with guns and other weapons.

Another face-off occurred on June 10, when Klansmen and Black protesters marched at the same time in the town square. More than 1,000 people in all participated in the marches and rallies. The entire Tupelo police department was out in force, heavily armed with rifles and shotguns. There were a few clashes between the Klansmen and protesters,

Black protesters march through Okolona, MS, while the KKK watches from the side.

but no one was seriously injured. Several people were arrested.

By this time, the protest had grown from the single complaint of police brutality into issues involving jobs, housing, and education. Most of the Black people living in Tupelo were poor. Black unemployment was significantly higher than white unemployment. Black civil rights activists began demanding better job opportunities and called for the hiring of more Black teachers and administrators, in addition to jobs in the police and fire departments.

The Protests Spread

On July 8, the most tense demonstration occurred when nearly 250 peaceful Black protesters marched through Tupelo. Groups of Klansmen glared at the marchers from parked pickup trucks and street corners. One Klansmen said they were only "monitoring to make sure no laws are violated." Police officers stood by in protective gear and carried shotguns during the hot, tense afternoon.

No violent clashes were reported on July 8, but the Tupelo marches spread to nearby Lexington, Okolona, Canton, and Corinth. Organized by the United League of Mississippi, Black protesters in these cities held marches, boycotts, and rallies to

Alfred "Skip" Robinson speaks to supporters at a rally in Mississippi.

protest police brutality and demand better economic opportunities. Watchful Klansmen attended nearly every event.

In Okolona, 20 miles from Tupelo, dozens of incidents of violence between Black people and the KKK and their supporters were reported in 1978. "There's more racism in Mississippi in 1978 than there was in 1962," said Alfred Robinson, president and founder of the United League.

The Equal Rights Amendment

While tensions boiled in the South, the fight for equal rights shifted to Washington, DC, where demonstrators marched for **ratification** of the Equal Rights Amendment (ERA) on July 9. The ERA is a proposed amendment to the U.S. Constitution that would guarantee equal legal rights for all Americans regardless of gender. It is intended to overturn many practices and state and federal laws that discriminate against women. If ratified, the amendment would give Congress the power to enforce its terms with legislation.

The first version of the ERA was written by Alice Paul and Crystal Eastman and introduced in Congress in 1923. The proposal was approved by the Senate in March 1972 and

Many demonstrators wore white in solidarity during the March for Equality.

MICHIGAN NOW

E.R.A. YE

Alice Paul (left) and Crystal Eastman (right) wrote the original ERA.

then sent to state legislatures for ratification. States had seven years to approve the proposal.

The July 9 "March for Equality" was at the time the largest demonstration in women's rights history. Organized by the National Organization of Women, more than 100,000 people marched on the nation's capital. More than 325 organizations sponsored the march, including labor unions and educational groups. Standing in 95-degree heat, marchers listened to more than 30 political and activist leaders speak in support of the ERA. The demonstration successfully achieved its main goal: Congress did indeed extend the deadline for ratification of the ERA until 1982.

Trudy Orris

Trudy Orris was one of the leading organizers and participants in the July 9 March for Equality. Born in 1916 in New York City to a poor Jewish family, Gertrude "Trudy" Orris was a prominent civil rights activist during the 1960s and 1970s. Orris became active in the American labor movement and worked as a **union** organizer in the 1930s. She became an advocate of the civil rights movement and served as head of the New York Parents of SNCC, a group supporting the Student Nonviolent Coordinating Committee. Orris hosted dozens of Black student activists from the South, arranging for housing, medical care, and fund-raising events. She often traveled to the South to participate in desegregation and Black voting rights demonstrations. Orris died in 2004 at age 88.

Trudy Orris (center) at a women's rights march in Washington, DC.

The Statue of Liberty is the site of a women's rights march in August 1978.

...LITY OF RIGHTS UNDER THE LAW SHALL NOT BE DENIED OR AB...
...THE UNITED STATES OR BY ANY STATE ON ACCOUNT OF...

Activists Dick Gregory and Betty Friedan at the March for Equality.

In 2020, the required majority of 38 states finally ratified the ERA. However, in order for the ERA to become an amendment, Congress must remove the 1982 deadline for ratification. As of September 2022, Congress has not eliminated the deadline. ■

A crowd gathers on the steps of the U.S. Capitol to protest anti-Indigenous legislation in Congress.

5

Victories

The First Amendment to the U.S. Constitution guarantees freedom of religion to all Americans. One might expect that the religious beliefs and practices of Indigenous Peoples would fall under the protection of the amendment. But for many years, federal and state laws have restricted the practice of Indigenous religions. Legislation prevented Indigenous groups from entering traditional holy lands and sacred sites. Laws also banned certain Indigenous religious dances. Some laws and other government actions even prevented Indigenous Peoples from using feathers in religious ceremonies.

By the late 1960s, the Indigenous civil rights movement, also called the American Indian Movement (AIM) was making its voice heard. AIM activists demanded control over tribal areas and the return of lands they believe were illegally

A woman paints a sign reading, "Indian American Land" during the occupation of Alcatraz.

taken by the federal government. The group also demanded protection of their legal rights, including the right to practice their traditional religions and culture. To publicize its cause, in 1969 AIM activists occupied the abandoned federal prison Alcatraz in San Francisco Bay, California.

Indigenous activists organize inside the federal prison at Alcatraz.

The Longest Walk

The Longest Walk helped raise awareness of the problems of Indigenous Peoples, including the lack of jobs and health care. The 2,700-mile walk across the country began with a few hundred people departing from Alcatraz Island in California in February 1978. More than 80 Indigenous tribes as well as white, Black, and Latino supporters participated in the march. On July 15, thousands of marchers entered Washington, DC, where they began a week of demonstrations and teach-ins to draw attention to problems faced by Indigenous Peoples. The journey also hoped to prevent passage of bills before Congress that would threaten Indigenous treaties and limit hunting and fishing rights. The Longest Walk was an inspiring success: None of the proposed legislation was ever passed by Congress.

A crowd of demonstrators assembles in Washington, DC, during the Longest Walk.

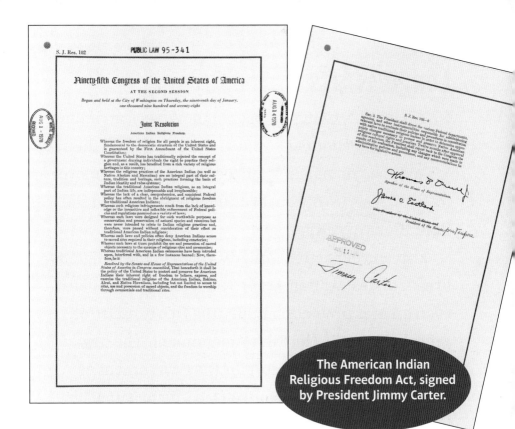

The American Indian Religious Freedom Act, signed by President Jimmy Carter.

The occupation of Alcatraz lasted 19 months, making international headlines. The bold act spurred the government to develop a policy of granting Indigenous groups more self-government. Millions of acres of tribal lands were restored to Indigenous groups, and increased government funding for Indigenous education, housing, and health care followed. The occupation also served as a powerful symbol of strength and unity for all Indigenous Peoples. Throughout the 1970s, Indigenous activists and their supporters continued to pressure the federal government to create laws to address their demands.

Congress Acts

On August 11, Congress passed the American Indian Religious Freedom Act (AIRFA) of 1978. While the act looked good on paper, it lacked the ability to enforce its laws. A series of court rulings demonstrated the limitations of AIRFA.

Fifteen years later, Congress passed the Religious Freedom Restoration Act of 1993. The law provided even greater protection under the free exercise of religion clause in the First Amendment. The new act makes it more difficult for the government or private businesses and citizens to infringe upon an individual's religious rights.

Navajo children study English at a school for Indigenous students in 1948.

Indigenous children arrive at the Carlisle Indian Industrial School in Pennsylvania around 1900.

Protecting Indigenous Families

The Indian Child Welfare Act (ICWA), enacted in November 1978, gave tribal governments exclusive power over children who live on a reservation. It also gives preference to Indigenous families in the adoption and foster care of Indigenous children. The act was a response to the nation's policies of removing Indigenous children from their families.

Protecting America's Mothers

On October 31, the Pregnancy Discrimination Act (PDA) became law to prohibit discrimination in the workplace "on the basis of pregnancy, childbirth, or related medical conditions." PDA includes discrimination in respect to hiring and firing, pay, promotions, and other aspects of employment. Companies with less than 15 employees are exempt from the act. The law was passed in response to the Supreme Court decision *General Electric Company v. Gilbert* (1976). In that case, the court ruled that an employer could exclude conditions related to pregnancy from employee sickness and accident insurance benefits plans.

PDA has enabled more pregnant women to continue working, and working longer, without being forced to leave their jobs. The law compels employers to treat a pregnant woman in the same way it treats a disabled employee. An employer is obliged to provide light duty, such as not lifting heavy objects, or not working with dangerous chemicals. Employers may have to provide different job functions or disability leave to pregnant employees.

The Pregnancy Discrimination Act amends Title VII of the Civil Rights Act of 1964.

From 1819 to 1969, the federal government operated nearly 500 boarding schools across the United States under the Federal Indian Boarding School Initiative. Government officials removed Indigenous children from their homes, often forcibly, and placed them in white boarding schools against parents' wishes. Many of the schools received support from religious institutions. Other times the government paid religious institutions to operate the boarding schools themselves. The government claimed its goal was to **assimilate** Indigenous children into white society. Critics of the program claimed the government's true aim was to erase Indigenous cultures entirely.

After the end of the boarding school program, the practice of separating Indigenous children from their families continued. In the 1970s, studies showed that about one-third of all Indigenous children were separated from their families by federal, state, and private child welfare adoption agencies. The children were placed in non-Indigenous adoptive homes, foster care, and educational institutions.

Though ICWA has shown positive results, Indigenous families are still four times more likely to have their children removed and placed in foster care than white families. ▪

A segregated bus in apartheid-era South Africa carries a sign reading, "Non-Europeans [meaning Black people] Only."

6

A Declaration for Humanity

On November 27, 1978, the United Nations Educational, Scientific and Cultural Organization (UNESCO) adopted the Declaration on Race and Racial Prejudice. The main idea of the declaration is that racism violates human worth and dignity. The declaration promotes the principle of equality and the rights of all human beings regardless of race, color, or nationality. All humans, it states, contribute to the progress of civilization. The declaration had wide support and was adopted by most nations.

The 1978 declaration was not the first UNESCO statement on racism and discrimination. In its duty to oppose any policy or instruction that promotes the inequality of

Declaration on race

and racial prejudice

adopted by
the General Conference of Unesco
at its twentieth session
Paris, 27 November 1978

unesco

The UN adopted
the Declaration on Race
and Racial Prejudice on
November 27, 1978.

races, UNESCO had already adopted four declarations dealing with race. The previous declarations were made in 1950, 1951, 1964, and 1967. Unlike previous declarations, however, the 1978 version addressed many aspects of racism, including cultural, economic, and political issues.

A signpost declares "WHITE AREA" along a bay in South Africa in 1976.

The Year in Sports

African American athletes made a big splash in the world of sports in 1978. In January, defensive end Harvey Martin of the Dallas Cowboys was named co-Most Valuable Player of Super Bowl XII. Martin shared the honor with teammate Randy White in the Cowboys 27–10 victory over the Denver Broncos.

On September 15, Muhammad Ali became the first heavyweight champion to win the title three times by defeating Leon Spinks in New Orleans. In November, Boston Red Sox outfielder Jim Rice was named American League Most Valuable Player (MVP), while Pittsburgh Pirates outfielder Dave Parker won the National League MVP. The year also witnessed Wendy Hilliard becoming the first African American member of the U.S. Rhythmic Gymnastics National Team.

Wendy Hilliard flying high at a gymnastics competition in 1986.

NET BLANKES
WHITES ONLY

Two Black people walk under a "WHITES ONLY" sign in South Africa in 1977.

Important Features of the Declaration

Article 4 of the declaration condemns racial segregation and apartheid specifically. In Article 6, the declaration says the State, or national government of a country, has the main responsibility to ensure human rights and basic freedoms. Article 9 expands on this concept, claiming special attention "should be paid to racial or ethnic groups which are socially or economically disadvantaged . . . in particular in regard to housing, employment, and health."

The Unified Black Movement

The *Movimento Negro Unificado* (MNU), or Unified Black Movement, was founded in Brazil in 1978 by Thereza Santos and Eduardo de Oliveira e Oliveira and other Brazilian activists. The founders were inspired by the civil rights movement in the United States. The organization was formed to end racial discrimination, police harassment, and Black underemployment and poverty in Brazil, the largest country in South America and the fifth-largest country in the world. The MNU successfully brought together several Black political groups, making the organization the most influential national civil rights group in Brazil.

The Unified Black
Movement in Brazil

1978–2002

ZUMBI VIVE

DAVID COVIN

David Covin's 2006 book examines the civil rights movement in Brazil.

The Susan B. Anthony silver dollar.

Women's Recognition

On December 13, 1978, the United States Mint in Philadelphia began stamping the Susan B. Anthony dollar coin, the first U.S. coin to honor a woman. During the 19th century, Anthony championed women's voting rights and worked to abolish slavery. The coin features a likeness of Anthony on one side and an American eagle landing on the moon on the other. This was not the year's first national honor for women activists. In February 1978, antislavery activist and Civil War veteran Harriet Tubman became the first Black woman to appear on a U.S. postage stamp. The stamp was part of the U.S. Postal Service's (USPS) Black Heritage USA series, the longest-running USPS series in history. ■

Harriet Tubman

Black Heritage USA 13c

The U.S. Postal Service stamp honors antislavery activist Harriet Tubman.

Marian Anderson receives the Congressional Gold Medal from President Jimmy Carter.

CONCLUSION

The Legacy of 1978 in Civil Rights History

The year 1978 was a landmark period when the activism of African Americans, Latinos, Indigenous people, women, and gay individuals made headlines. Their achievements built upon the civil rights movement of the 1950s and 1960s, expanding it to include other groups seeking a more equal role in American society. Women in particular made significant advancements, as the year featured many famous "firsts."

On December 3, 1978, opera and spirituals singer Marian Anderson became the first African American to receive a Kennedy Center Honor from the John F. Kennedy Center for the Performing Arts in Washington, DC. Anderson was one of five artists to be chosen as the first recipients of the Kennedy Center Honors. Anderson was a barrier-breaking figure in the fight for Black performers to overcome discrimination. In 1955, she became the first

African American singer to perform at the prestigious Metropolitan Opera in New York City. Among the many honors she won was the first Presidential Medal of Freedom in 1963 and the Congressional Gold Medal in 1977.

Women also made their mark in other key areas. In 1978, Jill Elaine Brown became the first African American woman pilot for a major U.S. passenger service, Texas International Airlines. Also in 1978, U.S. Navy nurse Joan C. Bynum became the first African American woman promoted to the rank of captain. Bynum's promotion opened the door for other women to break barriers in the U.S. military.

Jill Brown (center) receives congratulations to qualify for training as a military pilot in 1975.

Despite its noble goals, the 1978 UNESCO Declaration on Race and Racial Prejudice has not eliminated racism around the world. In September 2021, the UN General Assembly pledged to redouble its efforts to combat the problem, including harm caused by religious discrimination, specifically anti-Semitic, anti-Muslim, and anti-Christian prejudice.

Captain Joan C. Bynum in 1978.

From all walks of society, the activists and achievers of 1978 made their mark in the ongoing struggle for the equal rights and freedoms of all Americans. Their work continues today. ▪

Toni Morrison

Toni Morrison at the Carl Sandburg literary awards in Chicago, Illinois, in 2010.

Toni Morrison is one of the most celebrated authors in the world. Her novels, children's books, and plays have earned her many honors, including the Pulitzer Prize and Presidential Medal of Freedom. In 1993, Morrison became the first African American woman to win the Nobel Prize in Literature. The multitalented author has inspired new generations of writers and thinkers, and has helped shape African American culture.

Chloe Anthony Wofford—Toni Morrison—was born in 1931 in Lorain, Ohio, the second of four children born to George Wofford and Ramah Willis Wofford. Morrison was a good student and an avid reader. She starred on her high school debate team and was a member of the school's yearbook staff. After graduating from Lorain High School, Morrison moved to Washington, DC, to attend Howard University, a historically Black university. While at Howard, she began writing stories and changed her name to Toni.

Morrison takes a break from writing in New York City in 1979.

After graduating from Howard, Morrison continued her studies at Cornell University, where she earned a master's degree in English. She went on to teach English at Texas Southern State University and later Howard University. During her stay at Howard, Morrison met her husband, Harold Morrison. The couple had two sons.

While working as an editor for the Random House publishing company

"The function of freedom is to free someone else."

—TONI MORRISON

Morrison at Toronto's International Festival of Authors in 1982.

Morrison with her sons, Harold and Slade.

in Syracuse, New York, she completed her first novel, *The Bluest Eye*. In 1973, she published her second novel, *Sula*, which was nominated for the National Book Award in 1975. In 1978, her third novel, *Song of Solomon*, earned Morrison the celebrated National Book Critics Circle Award. Many critics and readers regard *Beloved*, her 1987 novel, as Morrison's finest work. The novel tells the story of a small Black town and urban communities over a period of 150 years. *Beloved* was awarded the

Pulitzer Prize for Fiction in 1988. From 1989 to her retirement in 2006, Morrison taught at Princeton University, where

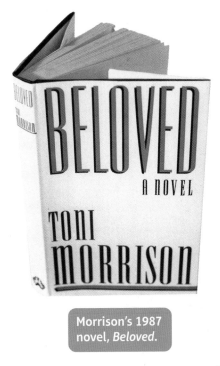

Morrison's 1987 novel, *Beloved*.

she developed programs to introduce students to writers and performing artists.

Morrison was one of America's most creative authors, writing essays, articles, plays, children's books, and nonfiction books. Much of her writing focuses on African American history and the Black experience in America. Many of the Black characters in her novels are struggling to find their own identity and self-worth. Her works often reference the Bible, which many readers believe gives her novels a spiritual

Morrison receives the Presidential Medal of Freedom from President Barack Obama.

Morrison at a book signing in London, England, in 2008.

aspect. Morrison's best works feature a main figure interacting with multiple characters, each with their own story and point of view.

Morrison died in 2019 at the age of 88. Oprah Winfrey was one of the speakers at Morrison's memorial. "Toni Morrison was her words, she is her words, for her words often were confrontational," said Winfrey. "She spoke the unspoken, she probed the unexplored. . . . Her words don't permit the reader to down them quickly and forget them, we know that. They refuse to be skimmed. They will not be ignored." ■

TIMELINE

The Year in Civil Rights

1978

Poland proposes the idea of a Convention on the Rights of the Child to the United Nations.

JANUARY 11

Toni Morrison receives the National Book Critics Circle Award for her third novel, *Song of Solomon*.

JANUARY 16

NASA names its first group of women astronauts and African American astronauts.

APRIL 8

Muhammad Ali addresses the United Nations Special Committee Against Apartheid.

JUNE 25

The rainbow flag of the gay rights movement flies for the first time at the San Francisco Gay Freedom Day Parade.

JULY 8

Activists march in Tupelo, Mississippi, to protest police brutality and demand better opportunities in jobs, housing, and education.

JULY 9

More than 100,000 demonstrators march on Washington, DC, for ratification of the Equal Rights Amendment.

AUGUST 11

Congress adopts the American Indian Religious Freedom Act of 1978.

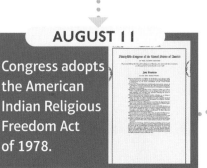

NOVEMBER

Congress adopts the Indian Child Welfare Act.

NOVEMBER 27

The UN adopts the Declaration on Race and Racial Prejudice, recognizing the value of all peoples to human civilization.

Declaration
on
race
and racial
prejudice

unesco

DECEMBER 13

The Philadelphia Mint begins stamping the Susan B. Anthony dollar, the first U.S. coin to honor a woman.

GLOSSARY

abolish (uh-BAH-lish) to put an end to something officially

activist (AK-tuh-vist) a person who works to bring about political or social change

affirmative action (uh-FUR-muh-tiv AK-shuhn) the use of policies, legislation, programs, and procedures to improve the educational or employment opportunities of certain groups to remedy the effects of long-standing discrimination against these groups

alienate (AY-lee-uh-nayt) to cause someone to feel isolated or alone

amendment (uh-MEND-muhnt) a change that is made to a law or legal document

apartheid (uh-PAHR-tide) in South Africa, a policy and system of segregation and discrimination on the basis of race

assimilate (uh-SI-muh-late) to absorb or integrate into a wider society or culture

boycott (BOI-kaht) a refusal to buy something or do business with someone as a protest

Chicano (chi-KAH-noh) an American, especially a man or boy, of Mexican descent

civilian (suh-VIL-yuhn) a person who is not a member of the military or police or firefighting force

civil rights (SIV-uhl rites) the individual rights that all members of a democratic society have to freedom and equal treatment under the law

comply (kuhm-PLYE) to act in agreement with rules or requests

decriminalization (dee-kri-muh-nuhl-ih-ZAY-shun) to remove or reduce the criminal status of

discrimination (dis-krim-uh-NAY-shuhn) prejudice or unfair behavior to others based on differences in such things as race, gender, or age

diversity (di-VUR-suh-tee) a variety

economic (ek-uh-NAH-mik) of or having to do with the way money, resources, and services are used in a society

federal (FED-ur-uhl) having to do with the national government, as opposed to state or local government

integrate (IN-ti-grate) to make facilities or an organization open to people of all races and ethnic groups

Jim Crow (jim kro) the former practice of segregating Black people in the United States

Ku Klux Klan (KOO kluks KLAN) a secret organization in the United States that uses threats and violence to achieve its goal of white supremacy; also called the Klan or the KKK

Latina/Latino (lah-TEE-nuh/lah-TEE-noh) a person of Latin American origin living in the United States

legislation (lej-is-LAY-shuhn) a law or set of laws that have been proposed or made

liberation (lib-uh-RAY-shuhn) the act of freeing someone or something from imprisonment, slavery, or oppression

lynching (LIN-ching) a sometimes public murder by a group of people, often involving hanging

picket (PIK-it) to stand or march outside a place in protest

plantation (plan-TAY-shuhn) a large farm found in warm climates where crops such as coffee, rubber, and cotton are grown

prejudice (PREJ-uh-dis) immovable, unreasonable, or unfair opinion about someone based on the person's race, religion, or other characteristic

prestigious (pres-TIJ-uhs) commanding great respect and status by being successful, powerful, rich, or famous

prohibit (proh-HIB-it) to forbid or ban something officially

ratification (ra-tuh-fuh-KA-shuhn) the act of signing or giving formal consent or approval to a law, treaty, or agreement

resolution (rez-uh-LOO-shuhn) a formal expression of opinion, will, or intent voted by an official body or assembled group

segregation (seg-ruh-GAY-shuhn) the act or practice of keeping people or groups apart

sit-in (SIT-in) a form of protest in which demonstrators occupy a place, refusing to leave until their demands are met

union (YOON-yuhn) an organized group of workers set up to help improve such things as working conditions, wages, and health benefits

BIBLIOGRAPHY

Duberman, Martin. *Stonewall*. New York: Penguin Books, 1993.

García, Mario T., and Ellen McCracken, eds. *Rewriting the Chicano Movement: New Histories of Mexican American Activism in the Civil Rights Era*. Tucson, AZ: University of Arizona Press, 2021.

Lerner, Natan. "New Concepts in the UNESCO Declaration on Race and Racial Prejudice." *Human Rights Quarterly*, Vol. 3, No. 1 (Feb. 1, 1981), 48–61.

Patterson, Robert J., ed. *Black Cultural Production After Civil Rights*. Chicago: University of Illinois Press, 2019.

Pious, Richard M., ed. *Civil Rights and Liberties in the 1970's*. New York: Random House, 1973.

Schultz, Debra L. *Going South: Jewish Women in the Civil Rights Movement*. New York: New York University Press, 2001.

Tuck, Stephen. "We Are Taking Up Where the Movement of the 1960s Left Off: The Proliferation and Power of African American Protest During the 1970s." *Journal of Contemporary History*. Vol. 43, No. 4 (Oct. 1, 2008), 637–654.

Selected Websites

https://www.history.com/this-day-in-history/song-of-solomon-wins-national-book-critics-circle-award

https://www.un.org/womenwatch/feature/iwd/1978/

https://www.nytimes.com/2017/01/26/theater/zoot-suit-a-pioneering-chicano-play-comes-full-circle.html

https://www.pbs.org/wgbh/americanexperience/features/zoot-rise-riots/

https://www.britannica.com/story/
   how-did-the-rainbow-flag-become-a-symbol-of-lgbt-pride

https://kansaspress.ku.edu/978-0-7006-1046-4.html

https://www.equalrightsamendment.org/the-equal-rights-amendment

https://www.nytimes.com/1978/07/09/archives/black-protest-is-
   monitored-by-klan-as-a-mississippi-boycott.html

https://www.washingtonpost.com/archive/politics/1978/06/26/
   tupelo/70732f78-2b16-46fc-be94-e1ab3d57f556/

https://www.mtsu.edu/first-amendment/article/1053/
   american-indian-religious-freedom-act-of-1978-as-amended-in-1994

https://www.nytimes.com/1978/12/04/archives/washington-honors-5-
   in-the-arts-personal-tributes-they-honor-us.html

https://www.nasa.gov/image-feature/1978-astronaut-class

https://www.washingtonpost.com/archive/lifestyle/1988/05/26/
   the-rise-and-dizzying-fall-of-max-robinson/61e675fb-a15b-4572-
   82f9-3f985a33cbab/

https://www.nationalgeographic.com/history/article/
   why-the-us-celebrates-womens-history-month-every-march

https://www.pbs.org/wgbh/americanexperience/features/
   zoot-enrique-henry-reyes-leyvas/

https://apnews.com/article/united-nations-general-assembly-
   africa-discrimination-race-and-ethnicity-racial-injustice-
   b1c65f0d54d93ad84aba0d7c65652609

INDEX

About the Author

Nel Yomtov is an award-winning author of nonfiction books and graphic novels about American and world history, geography, sports, science, mythology, and military history. He has written numerous titles in Scholastic's A True Book, Enchantment of the World, Cornerstones of Freedom, and Calling All Innovators series. Nel lives in the New York City area with his wife, Nancy, an educator. His son, Jess, is a sports journalist and website producer.

PHOTO CREDITS